EUMAEUS TENDS

Also by Richard Fenton Sederstrom

Fall Pictures on an Abandoned Road

Disordinary Light

Folly, a Book of Last Summers

EUMAEUS TENDS

by

Richard Fenton Sederstrom

Published by the Jackpine Writers' Bloc

Cover photograph by Richard Fenton Sederstrom
Published by the Jackpine Writers' Bloc
Edited by Sharon Harris
Layout and cover design by Tarah L. Wolff

$14.00
ISBN#: 978-1-928690-25-2

Dedication

To Carol Sederstrom and Nick Salerno as always and ever.
And to my children, my grandchildren, and my great-grandchildren,
those descendant promises for whom Eumaeus stands
as the metaphor: our genial ancestry and continuance.

And for Sharon Harris and Tarah Wolff
for their forbearance dealing with me through four books.

Acknowledgments

The author gratefully acknowledges the following anthology, journals, and magazines for their kind permission to reproduce the following poems:

20x20 Art & Words 2011, "Blue Chords, Blue Clouds."
Avocet, "Just Before Dawn," "Opuntia," "Prosthetics," "Message Returned."
The Blue Guitar Magazine, "Easing the Light," "Her Black Hair," "In Asphodel Meadows," "Junco," The Poem as Ears, A Duet" also "Penelope" (a group of seven poems, including "Proem and Epilogue: Oar," "Her Warrior," "Their Child," "Penelope Rex," "Penelope and Odysseus," "Nobody's Son," "Envoi: Circe Circles"), "Kite Fishing at a Public Park," "Three Choruses for Mockingbird."
Friends Journal, "Meek," "Silences."
*Passager, "*Endlessly Rocking, *"*"Those Who Turned Back from the Mountain."
Plainsongs, "Strangers, Maybe."
Red Owl, "Afterwards."
South Ash Press, "Moon."
The Talking Stick, "County 40," "A Gaud for Our Well-Being," "Ice-Out," "Our Hands."
Unstrung, "Answer First, then Question," "Demodocus Deposes from a Rocky Hill in Arcadia," "Eumaeus Tends," "Epic and Hearth," "The Ivory Gate" (orig. "Drought in Ithaca"), "Laertes," "Metamorphoses: Narrators," "On Calypso," "Owl," "Soliloquy by the Candle Light of Day," "What You May Be Looking For."

Italicized inner quotations are taken from Robert Fagles' translation of *The Odyssey,* save for that on p. 45, which comes from George Chapman's translation. (The author's italics.)

A note from the poet: Thanks to Rebecca Dyer, I think that all of the sequence that I have taken to calling "Eumaeus Tends" has been published, either in *The Blue Guitar* or, now, in *Unstrung.*

Contents

3. Those Who Turned Back from the Mountain

4. Old Poet: New Prologue

EUMAEUS TENDS

How to Read the Poems

What You May Be Looking For

If you've been there many times before—
Noticed that the corpse of old adobe
Wall is maybe a little lower, weaker,
Bits of ancient straw sticking out
Like a boy's cropped hair or maybe
A very old man's scarce colorless whiskers—
Maybe just kicking around with your boot
You may learn to sense what you might
Be looking for, even if you're not looking
Much for anything—especially then.
If you sense what you're looking for
You will nudge with your boot
A ragged tooth of ancient pottery.

You pick it up, sense its familiar desert
Roughness, a patina between your fingers.
The shard is gray, almost a triangle
Rounded and with a bit of old rim.
The shard is bare for a thumb-nail width
Under eroded remains of the bulge of rim
And the bulge of lips that caress the jar
That the small shard had been with the thirst
To which the lips were indifferent.
But the water in the jar! The cool intimacy.

The jar of permeable half-fired clay
Is cool from evaporation of the film of water

That almost glazes the outside of it,
Which beneath that smooth band
Is pressed in by the potter's finger-nails
Small quarter-moons of indentation

That inscribe rows incised into the clay—
I see two rows on the shard.
I try to unravel my own thirst now
Lifting to my lips the story of our thirst together,
How we came to be so thirsty together,
The cactus-shriveled droughts we have shared,
The diminishing heft of the clay jar
As we pass it from lip to lip,
Word for word, look and stroke.

We sit, you and I under the reed-thatched
Roof of our ramada braced upon a circle of adobe wall,
Waiting for the sun to quaver into darkness,
The air to cool. Night and coyotes sing.
Bare feet leave departing prints in moon-lit sand.
Leave the pottery shard in place, its place,
Now that you sense what you are looking for,
Your place, the place you start from.

Easing the Light

When you flick on the light, you flick on the light only.
You don't think, don't need to.
But thinking is control, you know, which
You lose in the unthought flick of the switch
To the silent, masterly surge of blind lightning.

With a candle, even a brief stub, maybe only
A stub from the neglected rear of a kitchen drawer,
You control the light, control all that the light controls.
Your hand controls the light-defying wind,
While you illuminate the secret map of your palm.

With the oil lamp you accept the laws of control
That come from having to buy the oil,
Having to bring home the oil along the paved road,
The oil-paved road going back to gravel
In the gentle imprecise control of memory.

But when you have shut the door,
Have allowed the outside to darken, have lighted your will,
Then you fill the lamp in the resin-scented,
Fire-scented old kitchen, your grandparents' maybe
Or theirs. You trim the wick.

You light the lamp.
You adjust the wick for the light correctly controlled
To the brightness and the dimness you need
To control time to the needs of your soul,
And you open the book to light the poem.

The Poem as Ears, a Duet

for Jim Wenzel, tutor of old to my eyes and ears

After you have finished
With the contrariness of my recent poems,
And I know that of all people you will,
You may ask again what is the use of poetry,
And I hope you do.

I was over there picking raspberries again—
But there aren't so many over there this year—
When I looked toward a little rise
And I saw two pair of the biggest ears I have ever seen!

Because I have a new answer for you,
And this time it comes from your own eyes:

I couldn't help looking at how huge
Those ears were!
Then their heads rose above the undergrowth
And showed them to be two fawns, still spotted.

A poem may be as awkward
Looking as the ridiculous ears
On the popped-up heads of the two fawns you saw,
To remind us again how real the startling moment was then,

How real the startling moment is again
In the fragile magic of words,

How real the startling promise of the fawns,
Their ears, the words,

And the real, *real* promise of that grace of being,
Summoned to return to your own eyes
And our ears again and again.

But I still can't get over how huge
Those two pair of ears were when I first saw them.
The ears must have to grow fast for their survival

Just like our ears, the ones that hear inside
For our survival.

1. Just Before Dawn

Three Choruses for Mockingbird

It is six fifteen and the sun has almost rounded the last corner
Before the anguish of horizon.
The alarm we set to spice the errands of our retirement
Has awakened me.

No.
It has reminded me that I have lain awake,
No, that I have lain here in bed
Sometimes waking

Sometimes wondering why I am awake and why
I cannot go back to true sleep, blissfully remming away.
And I hear the mockingbird again
Peeping, chirping, cheeping, whirring

Peep peep peep
Chirp chirp chirp
Cheep cheep cheep
Whirr whirr whirr

Liiiiisten to the mockingbird
Liisten to the mockingbird
Liiisten to the mockingbird
Peeping chirping cheeping whirring

Triads over and over and over again
For love!
For love for love for love
!   !   !

2

How shall I contain my anger
Who have been awakened
Out of the black clot of night by crows
Cawing their rude schemes of language,

Generations of wrens' angry demands
In their shrill joy at formal
Separation from the seasons
Of my inexcusable intrusions,

Woodpecker in brain-defying counterpoint
To woodpecker
Hammering on a cabin wall
Another on a metal sign

Or the eagle,
No, the eagle's prey
Screaming its way into the machinery of talons,
Into the appetite of dark evolution?

3

How shall I, so angered now, who have been so enriched
By the Other voice than the song of the bird—
Be angered by the love choruses of the mockingbird
And not hear, a creature with so many appetites myself,

That they are also love songs? How shall I
Turn from the sleeping figure of my wife next to me,
Awakened, angry to be sure, but
Awakening back into love?

Into love?
Into love!
Into love!
Into love!

Atonement

Crow yak, yak, yaks
Sun rises

Sun rises
Crow yak, yak, yaks

Crow knows that he has brought up the sun
Sun knows that he has brought up the crow

I lie here under my good wool blanket
Having brought up the sun, the crow, and myself

I will lie here for a while, swarmed by this cacophonous triad
Then I will reach for a pencil and atone for the brightness, the noise
        and the affront.

Kite Fishing at a Public Park

For only this flight of moment it is a sleek
Small kite and we can almost see a thin string,
A deception, as always, of control.

But then the kite breaks away,
A kite unstrung, not fluttering
As we think it should, but unseeled,

Snatches the bait that a boy had barbed
To his line's end. A second boy casts
At the park pond, and a second kite,

A Mississippi kite, dives with hawk
Speed, hawk grace, hawk luck,
To the invisible bait and not the hook,

And glides away, leaves behind in that grace
An awed circle of small boys unaware
Now that mere fins ever were, bird-fisherboys

Enchanted, flashing thin whips
Of fishing rod, casting again and again
Above the little ring of lake, waving on

Sleek winged falcons sliding on air
Above them in figures and flourishes
Impossible to invent or train.

Kites swoop out of the noontide sun
At the very peak of the tent of sky, pluck bait
From hooks with impossible dexterity

And miraculous balance in our instinct
For passion at the chase in a flash,
All in aerial teasing, and soar above

Picnickers loafing on the grassy slopes
Of what was only a small town park
Before we flew by, hungry for grace.

Silences

Jim drops by to tell me
that he has seen an owl
in an aspen toward the end of our road.
I am listening to Mozart's Prague Symphony.

But it isn't that he saw the owl
even though it is only mid-afternoon in a hot sun.
It is that he heard the owl fly off,
that is he heard from the owl in flight a clarity of silence.

He mentions in passing the old truth that the owl
is the only bird that can fly in a wisdom of wing-composed silence.
The symphony ends a few minutes later,
flies off in its own wisdom to the Prague of my mind

in the composed silence of its final note.

Opuntia

Cactus blossoms—
waxy yellow profusion of prickly pear on the bajada,
purple flowers of staghorn cholla at the rim of the wash

smell only from a polite distance, subtly sweet, almost sweet.
Subtle.
Subtler. Stop. Stay where you are and let your nose work
without your brainish interference.

Subtle. But not if you get too close, if you
stick your nose where it is only the business
of bees, of bats to go.

Cactus blossoms appeal to your modesty.
So if you have none
gather your wealth.
Reap power. These

passing fragrances are not for you.

On the Dunes

Slalom tracks from last night's sidewinder—
some little drama of appetite
some kangaroo rat may have lived
to tell about or may have not.

But not to tell you and me
stopped here in the sand wondering.
The rat is well on into the motive for his leap back
into a night that stays to frighten only us.

Just Before Dawn

Just before dawn in the gray lamp
of the final pulse of moonlight

creosote bush
twisted mesquite

and something else
something

some things
brimless heads of somethings buried

round and gentle as lumps in the old mattress
ruthless as the broken springs that stab

through flophouse-blue stripes
in the old mattress cover

will if I turn my waking eyes from their terrible comfort
disappear into the harrowing new light

Junco

The junco at the side of the path
will multiply
in an explosive trice
and does—to a dozen or so—
smudged gray like the cloud-stuffed sky.
Then it is a promenade
of a tiny second's stately process
before they take to their tails.

Staid white chevrons slap
into a chaos of lunatic
precision. That gray and pudgy
sky and the gray and pudgy
poet hum into laughter. The gray
and pudgy birds hear this
of course and in pure silliness
we take off all over again. Consider

your own girth and grayness.
Take flutter.
Fly in sacred place.

Prosthetics

Is it a dogwood, looking so dogged
From where I sit behind a large pane of clear wisdom
Protected here in an air conditioned autumn—not fall
And not out there beyond my comfort—

Not *out* where the dogged dogwood,
The one I think is maybe an ash
But anyway an ash that has failed
To grasp the meaning of its being,

Out there in the confused fall so glassily opposed
To the autumn where I sit and stare
Because its upper story of leaves is all brown,
All the post-equinox margin of fall.

But its understory is still August green
And the tree itself is trying so hard
To figure out outside what it is doing
And what is happening to it when all the other trees—

The oak, the birch, the aspen, the poplar,
The rest of the world of leafiness is just so
Confused as is the dogged ash
By a fall that is partly over and partly not begun,

While I sit here in my own falling foliage
Incubated in the air-conditioned autumn
Where I can't see the green dying of leaves,
The evolving fenlands of distant tundra.

Stepping off the Kraton

Near Panorama Point, Nebraska

Below my feet, not far by greater standards than mine
Lies the impenetrable fossil of what is left
Of the oldest mountain on the continent.
How many thousands of millions of years
Did the geologist say?

Not all that far west and a bit south
Is Dinosaur National Park
Its famous clutter of giants' bones
Plastered into a vertical stratum
Like a bas-relief in gray gesso

One hundred and fifty million years old
Give or take a few hundred
Thousand human generations.
Under all the oceans no one
Has found fossil-bearing rock older than this.

I will turn my eyes from this glare of the recent,
Return my attention to the stable foolscap
Of unerodible foundation, solid
As my grandfather's stories, base rock
Into which my memories impress my eroding future.

Ice-Out

Worn tectonic plates four inches thick
Melting into cold slush,
Grays under a bulbous pewter sky.
I dream awake to such metallic violence

Erupted out of that chilly metaphor of continental
Thrust and succumbing wet movement
Sliding back and forth atop
The inviting depth of heat,

But only because I said what I said
To myself and my pen and the smooth ice
Of white paper.
For

It is only a lake surface,
White ice shifting with wind plowing
A cracked surface to slide over
A gentle gray force of old and tender ice,

All no more violent than seasonal melt,
No less tender than Earth's roiled surface
In Earth's ancient seasons of ice
Thaw and renewal

And renewal.

End of Days on Turtle Island

Half keeled over in the fall drought
An abandoned rowboat hangs by mooring ropes
From an abandoned dock. The dock is gray
From use and weather. The water is gray.

A great gray snapping turtle burrows
At the mud below inches of chilling water
Between the boat's naked hull
And the moribund weeds on the lake bottom.

The ice that will tear the fabric of the boat
Will chill the turtle far beyond its cold blood.
The ice surge will drag the wooden dock posts
In twisted splinters back and forth and out.

The rowboat will wait until spring
Before it finishes drowning.
The silent Earth of turtle will be freed
To slide out, then down into the house of teeth.

Subjectory

This sinking gray bubble of clogged feathers
on the surface of Shallow Lake,
water-logged feathers of blue heron
only a quarter of the corpse
above the surface now,
three quarters down aimed toward the adventure
of sinking forever.

Its spindle legs fulcrum its appetites no more
nor is its triggered beak any danger
to frogs or minnows or baby ducks and loons—
or perch or bluegill or rock bass
once indifferent to living,
now guaranteed their red gills for some life more.

The cartridge of head, matted plume, bullet of beak
aim the rest of the bird down
where its gray disguise will disappear
entire into the masking muck beneath
the lily pads and cabbage weed.

Bubbles of methane
signaling the blue heron's slow entry into
the afterworld of gray peat—
oil, coal, immortality
or new fire—new gray ash
a nativity of loam.

2. Eumaeus Tends

Eumaeus Tends to Livestock and Voices

Eumaeus is encumbered by a narrative mind,
a ghost-voice of more than a few pasts. He thinks mostly
when he is speaking—to his pigs, to himself,
to whatever god is least likely to be listening,
to his master's ancient dog, asleep or not, and in speaking,
mostly he tells.

                You talk, Eumaeus.

It was in talking of your master one day that you asked
your customary audience about the condition of Ithaca.
Not that you cared.

When you first meet her what is Penelope doing?
She is ruling Ithaca. And she is ruling not by force but,
as Odysseus does in his life, by cleverness, the way
her husband would have done the job had he not been gulled,
mostly by himself, into the corporate imperium
of Agamemnon & Bro.

                Penelope
has got so far desperate as to treat her beloved son
Telemachus with the cold eye of the ruler. She knows
that if the suitors believe Telemachus means nothing
to his mother and queen, they might not kill him.

Then Eumaeus asks,
and this time he seems to have addressed the poet,
maybe Demodocus, maybe some future old poet,

When you first meet him, Poet, what is Odysseus doing?

Odysseus is weeping. Odysseus is weeping
helplessly for Penelope. Odysseus has lived
for seven years in a delirium of happy dying:
wine, woman, song. More woman. And he has been
promised immortality, outside time, too far outside desire,
for wine, woman, song, and more and more woman.
But Odysseus sits on a crag overlooking the sea,
weeping for Penelope.

Homer, the Odysseyan mind who invented the Odysseyan
mind, switched the traditional roles for man and woman.
The woman will understand the life of the man,
having lived it: defiant in the face of certain defeat,
iron-willed, determined. The man will understand
the life of the woman, having lived it: dependent, vulnerable,
trained to weep for the inevitable human losses.

The great tale of more-than-romantic love reaches
its climax at their moment of reunion, the suitors gone,
the blood mopped up, nothing for the ageing couple to do
but size each other up finally and make do with what
they are given, or what they have left to give each other.
Like the rest of us.

Odysseus is seated on a stool.
He leans his back against a pillar resting from a trying morning.
Penelope approaches him, then stops short. Telemachus chides
her for not going to her husband ("you are always cold").
But Odysseus stops him, letting him know that Penelope
will come to him when she is ready.
If she means to test him more, it is her choice to do so.

Odysseus has figured out what allows us to be in love
and to be loved: the wonderment of Choice.
Penelope has her way with the famous trick about the bed.
Penelope no longer needs to know who Odysseus is,
only what Odysseus may have become, and she needs,
for their life together, to find out. She finds out.

Besides maybe Demodocus, a good number of voices
agreed to appear in Eumaeus' chattering mind:
the distant people of ancient Achaea of course,
and some onetime residents of places like Minneapolis
and maybe some other poleis, and sometimes maybe
even voices that happen to the poet along the way
as voices will create themselves—even, sometimes, the poet's.

But the voice that volunteered most strongly is Eumaeus,
un-traveled slave who has been content to raise pigs and wait
for Odysseus to return. Maybe he is waiting. He may not know.

The fate of Achaea is shrouded, hinted at through the woeful fate
of non-returning veterans of the Mycenaean grand folly.
Telemachus and his Ithaca are statistics for archeology.
Nor do we know what happened to Eumaeus, but Eumaeus

is only a swineherd and a slave, not even a peasant.
We don't need to know what happens to Eumaeus, save
that we know him to be a man who understands the skills
of abiding. Eumaeus is the us of non-history. We are the us
who have survived, so far, as Eumaeus could tell us, in order
to keep the tales alive and moving.

        Careful Eumaeus,
you are the one left to assist us to remember the voices of the poetry,
when no god is listening. While the gate of horn is open, speak.

In Asphodel Meadows

Junco is a traveling bird.
He travels north of where I sit right now.
He travels south of where I sit right now but
He does not travel *to* where I sit right now, reminding me
That *I* need not travel to where I sit right now
Nor may I be where I sit right now if like Junco
I choose to fly and still be
Where I sit right now.

I can travel to Junco if I wish.
I can learn to spot Junco
In his chosen spot in the woods if I choose
And Junco has license to adventure in his regard to me.
It is a kinship of the distant sort that I most desire most days.
Junco and I have such color of freedom to share
Sharing the gray of our years such philosophy of freedom
That one of us has learned how much the matter is
Of where he knows he is and where he knows he isn't.

We have learned in our travels from meadow to meadow
Or from corner to edge of some meadow
The virtue of sharing our minor secrets
With our timely cousin not too far removed,
The sojournal asphodel lovely to behold,
Sempiverdant in her seasons only here—grave keeper
Of secrets we three share that often where we are
Is not where we are but

In the meadow or wood between the meadows where
The three of us spend so many of our untimely hours
Together or apart
Or apart and apart together.

Epic and Hearth

Who knows who invented comedy?
A thrown spear wobbles harmlessly
Off the flank of a charging aurochs.
The aurochs narrowly misses
The spear thrower, who, avoiding
The aurochs' natural response,
Falls into the muddy fen, where
Instead of drowning, he flounders
Covered in mud. His mates laugh.
He stares at them. Then he laughs.
But it isn't comedy yet. At night,
Around the fire, meatless again,
They talk of the day. They work off
The day's frustrations talking.
The spear thrower, the man who
Is the cause of their hunger, tells again
What happened. The wobbly spear,
The prat-fall, the mud. He stands
As he tells the story and imitates the fall,
The sputtering, the image of mud.
That's where the comedy is made.

The Greeks, we can be pretty sure,
Invented tragedy, by way of having
Invented the hero—Theseus, Perseus,
Jason, Heracles, Oedipus, Achilles.
Inventing the hero, they invented

Conscience, which the hero in his deeds,
Or after them, because of them, lacks.
But it is Homer, least tragic, most
Understanding of imaginations, who
Invented the Greeks. So what does that
Make of the hero, of tragedy, of Greeks,
Of us? Penelope and Odysseus take
Each other to that sacred bed again,
Make love. In the morning they'll awaken,
Make love again, sleep a while longer.
After they finally rise, they'll say Good
Morning to Telemachus. All three
Will have breakfast. Talk. Plan the day.
Then they'll all go out and deal
With some legacies, handle the politics,
Plan a leisurely trip to the underworld,
Buy some boating gear, an oar or two, or
Sit back of an evening telling the old tales.
Always, someone, some longing one
From the oarless fens perhaps, is willing to listen.

Proem and Epilogue: Oar

The returned is no longer himself.
What was broken in her is no mystery.
What may be broken in him is still rooted
In his longing.

Longing, he is driven to be whole again.
Longing for her, his only wholeness
Must be the two connected in that myth,
Those roots . . . Earth.

She looks back at the bronze sword,
Broken on the bleeding floor,
Looks,
Before returning to his eyes,

Out at the standing ships, sails furled,
Sees the banked oars
Ready for sea again,
Returns his look and knows.

Her Warrior

The day he left, face disguised by the helmet he wore then,
Because he had no arms unencumbered to carry it seemingly,
Untied chin strap flapping, his awkward bronze sword
In the belted, studded leather scabbard slung over his left shoulder,

Ammo belt over his right, olive green duffle
Dangling from under his slung plated armor,
All slipping, leather and bronze, supple and burnished,
Over the right shoulder a sheaf of spears,

Bronze tipped, glinting in the tide-hurrying sun,
Like the proud glint of his untried cleverness.
And I saw. And was what?
Saddened and somehow delighted at once,

A seed of this longing these twenty years.
He had tied them too loosely, the spears,
Hadn't balanced them on his blistering shoulder,
Hadn't considered the weight of the forward ends,

So that they threatened to pitch into the path before him,
As they splayed around like an ill-bound sheaf of stalks in the field.
He nearly tripped then, looked about to see me again
And those old mariners too, his trusting . . .

How hard they had practiced away their natural doubt,
The men not looking, seeming not to be watching.
He hopped a little when he readjusted to a wooden chatter,
A clanking, a tooth-grinding squeak of oiled leather.

The outward look of what should have been his first test
Of warrior poise, the last pose of his manly apprenticeship,
Laertes looking on critically, distant,
Chest puffed in fatherly pride, all disdain, and a tear.

I saw that he was still a boy; I a girl.
I swallowed and held out my hand to the glittering sea,
I waved, not, I almost hoped, the full goodbye.
These fingertips were smooth then,

Uncalloused by my years of pushing the needle,
Pulling thread . . . in, out . . . then out, in,
The beat of my heart, pace of breath,
Pattern of our loving consummated pulse.

In, out—pride, longing, love, loneliness.
This practiced pulse of weaving the tapestry,
These many hued strands of finger-biting wool,
The pulse too, of decision, of wifely obeisance,

Of governing on the sly, of motherhood,
Of keeping the secret kingship, of ruling without ruling,
Learning to deceive, too seldom free for interruption
Or completion by that other pulse, the longing.

What of Ithaca, abandoned now to Wall Street,
Flesh-faced lust for cargoes of full amphorae,
For resigned comfort, fat bellies turned from the fall?
What of the child, only incarnation from our cosmos-rooted bed?

Their Child

Two discolored sheets of paper
At the top of the heap
Of scoria left over from living
Reduced to the sifted ash of evidence—

Imitation parchment marriage license,
Yellowed certificate—High School Social Studies—
Unused for fifty years,
Yellowed paper as virgin as
Your bland courses abandoned
But saved at the top of your cargo,

The very pick of scuttled treasure—
Your need to protect your own from the dire
Wolf of ordinary wants, happiness,
The desperate continuity of husbandry,
The teaching,
The music you loved,

Your library of Classical 78s all discarded, given
To a stranger on a whimsical gesture
Of what terrible pain?—
Cables cut.
The voyage . . .

Your voyage, my drift.
Too far apart

Or too close not to be apart?
You too far in love
Not to sacrifice passion for position,
I too far in passion to be able to love.

Who on his own
Has ever really known who gave him life?
They say I am his son.
I am hers. *Why do you spurn my father so?*

Laertes

In her room in the house of her husband
Her fine knuckles chafe and crack.
Her fingertips harden with the push of the needle
In, out, a breathing in the bare linen
That informs the web of shroud. For whom?

Yes. I know.
It is good to know that one has a daughter
To care for the public abstractions of dotage and dying.
In and out.

The needle through the embroidered cloth
The needle of breath
In and out of lungs patínaed
With the dust of these hills.

Days of too much living, if living alone is living
And not breath-borne ash of memory—
All longing these decades past—
Eurycleia young again!

The hands. Hers. Mine.
Here are hands that have gripped the sword, the bow,
The reins of chariot horses, even—

For what does it matter to a man at the settled helm
Of ruling—the handles of a plow,
The shepherd's crook. The butcher knife.

The hands hold nothing now, or nothing well
Save to support the brow above them in its dozing

Like my grandfather
When the fragile support of his ill-formed cosmos
Threatened to drop his attic treasures down on him,
The stuffed owl he bought one Friday
In a Minneapolis bar—
One of the lazy Fridays before the depressions, outer and inner.

The fingers grasp nothing, fumble with a spoon
Ladling gruel to palsied lips
Open to the invisible wisp of a regal wave
Or princely salute to seafarers and soldiers
Sailing for Troy, errands for the corporate imperium.

Only five generations down from the creative prick of Zeus,
Odysseus sacrificed now forever
To the foam of Uncle Poseidon's rabid fancy.

Telemachus, doomed by birth, by his wandering sire,
By his grandfather's faithless devotion to inheritance—

Your mother is king now, boy, by my indecision.
Let me not be mad. My hand.

I shall not look upon hers, withering at her embroidery
The shroud of my only hope. I embroider this . . .

Telemachus, grandson doomed to be my heir, not his,
Only maybe doomed to survive inheritance,
I have loved too cannily for passion.

Your passion would weave the shroud
Of your mother's cryptic love.
                              Who on his own
Has ever really known who gave him life? you ask.

Look around.

It's the unborn old poet gives us life. Death. Life.
Why do you spurn my father so?
You may well ask again.

Owl

The image is apt, I suppose. It was
Like an attic in there, cluttered with the discards
From his self-indulged permanent adolescence,
Despoiling farmers' daughters, turning Chaos into chaos.

Worse, it *was* an attic, in a Minneapolis summer,
Humid, smelling of the detritus and sweat
Of forgettable generations, sloughed skin,
The skin of mortals that they cannot slough,

That swallows them whole, so exhausted
That it can neither digest nor protect its meal,
The piteous aliment of human innards.
The Great Head smelled of his duplicitous playtimes,

Of humans clawing with bloody nails
At the delusionary privilege of being what he is—
Zeus! Once out of that turbulent crucible
It is better to be an owl, even a stuffed one.

On Calypso

If she hadn't been immortal,
Hadn't been made immortal,
Hadn't been made—

Poiésis, a bricolage of doldrum yearning—
I should have traveled all the farther,
Traveled to Dido, immortal too perhaps

In the Kalliopean throes of her mortality,
The incessant torment of breathing—
If she hadn't been immortal,

If she had been Dido instead
I should have been enthralled not
By her lust but by my own.

But what of Penelope *then*?

Penelope Rex

My little man.
How can she honey the hard bread of his nightmare days
Even to tell him what dream he's in?
You're the man of the house now—

And more Nobody now than the maker of tricks
No trick in his own repertoire
No repertoire but . . .
You've got to be brave

Let Mother alone with her housework, her weaving—
That web, strung, unstrung,
The plot ravels, unravels as her only control
The tapestry of his errand must never unravel—

A man now, my little man, my big man—
Must travel; his princely chiton
Declares manhood, disguises only who he is,
Nobody the Second,

He whoever among mortals
Is most unblest—
Disguises also what he must not know
His mother's marriage license

His death warrant.
He would die if he knew

Only maybe at someone else's hand.
My big man of the house . . .

Of woman, enigma.
No epic but mother-story,
The she-trickster's own funhouse of dire necessity,
A chilled triad of suspended love.

Metamorphoses: Narrators

"You remember all the things that never happened"

The stories. Laestrygonians, Lotus Eaters, Calypso.
That bag of winds. Only stories.
And they all know that.
I know that. Only stories. And the teller is meant
To tell them as though they were true.

There's been agreement about that
Almost since stories became stories
And not reports of neighborhood gossip
Even from far distant neighborhoods.
Stories are like this:

The better they get the more spectral they become.
Certainly the teller doesn't regard them as factual.
Well, maybe the Cyclops bit. Maybe.
Polyphemus of less than distant memory.
Maybe.

It is hard when you begin to lose the original mood
The terror that gets lost in the telling and retelling
As the terror grows in the listeners
In the telling and retelling.
To lose that in yourself means to lose the single
Fact in the story
The original witness of it.

So the storyteller
At the mercy of his listeners
The mercy of what the storyteller
Learns to know of the listeners' natural apprehensions

And misapprehensions,
The ambiguity of anticipation—

The storyteller begins to filter all this into the story,
Even perhaps Polyphemus, the one-eyed
(*Oh! The Wine!*) Giant.
Even *he* fades into the old features
And he becomes truer and truer
And truth begins to lie

Not in the memory or in the story itself
But in the story's future, where its truth *must* lie.
Truth lies the more it is truth.
Fading before him in the mists of telling
Nausicaa is born all dream.

Penelope too.
But *out* of the story
Penelope is as sound as his soundless longing for her.

Eumaeus Tends

The old dog will come back or he will not.
It does not matter,
Not to the dog, not to me.
Not to my pigs.

If they were sheep. Sheep are different.
With sheep the dog has two choices.
The dog will herd the sheep. Or
The dog will kill a sheep. Maybe two.

With pigs it is different.
No dog will herd pigs. Pigs won't stand for it.
No dog will kill a pig. Dogs know the danger.
Especially an old dog. Especially this old dog.

He will come back though, unless he has died.
I think he won't die.
If it were me . . . but I have young dogs.
I don't need this dog.

Pigs almost never stray from the trough.
A pig far from the trough will either starve
Or he will learn to kill the biggest dog.
The dog doesn't need me. In me

The dog has no one to die for, no one to live for. So.
The dog will return. And if
After these years the master himself should return
Then the dog can make his choice.

He will choose to see the master, or
He will choose to die. Or some god will choose.
With me, the dog has no reason to choose.
He will come back.

And I?
I will save the fattest pig for the master.
Then I will make my choice.
Or I will not.

Afterwards

She watches him hunched
Exhausted on a bare stool shoved back in a bare corner,
Sweat-clogged back braced tightly against a cold pillar,
Watches, knows who he is by now, surely,
But, surely as well, not what he has become,
Twenty years down time,

Awash in brine and blood and rumor, legend, fear—
His reality the casual treachery
Of the first modern man.
He appears in the ragged, smelly guise
Of a village lowlife,
Flanked by two of the same wretched brotherhood.

And the son stands by blankly, wondering,
Why does she not move?—
Watching too.
Go to him, Mother . . .
Because the son, having held the quiver for him,
Even taking the loyal peril of fledgling squire
With a spattered bronze weapon of his own—

Aghast too, and awed
By the fighting,
The deaths, the blood of the old warrior
Hot in his own untested form—
A man now who has never been a boy.
You were always cold, Mother . . .
Always, but he must not know, his father.

Penelope and Odysseus

All his trials over but one,
He returns the texture of her apprehension.
The cold gaze retires softly for him, he fondly
Shifting the weary, taut slump, residue

Of his hero's flexed posture, sitting
Against that pillar, nothing flexed but his own apprehension—
Dripping bronze sword still and always unsheathed
Like his hero's meager conscience,

But the sword exiled now from this new decorum
Only waiting to be cleaned by who still live of the servants,
No longer a weapon—a mere utensil
Of obsolete manliness.

All corpses dragged off to parents and pyre,
He sees into her, knows this is not mere death,
But life for the first time in twenty years, the essential,
Terrifying generation of continuance.

She looks at him from this self-imposed refraction of distance
And one last question, the unspoken challenge
This time asked so far before language
That no syllables can save or staunch her instant desire.

She moves with the seasons of their stable cosmos
And with their lives, all stable because movement

Is visible, and she touches the thread of it.
Her hand is visible as it spins and unspins—

The moving web, out and in, out and in, back
And forth like the sea, like Odysseus in their bed,
Like Odysseus in her undulating memory, rooted
Like the hard knots of olive into the moving rock—

Caress and lunge, caress and lunge, weaving,
Unweaving, always the movement of hands, of limbs,
Of memory, surges of grief, palpitations of returning heat
Unanswered for so long. Now.

Himself again, not hero, not king, only self again,
The bond he had forsaken, she has forsworn
In the whirl of recognition.
No one moves again in the cosmic adventure.

Olive tree, bound into the unshifting
Earth Dance of memory. Blood
Of rooted Earth, blood of olive,
Oil beyond mere living—oil, blood, unction,

Union, one rootbound, guided in moving swift
Close cycles. Patterns glide, charioted
Round and round their sweat-glistened fecund unmoving
Earth—

Nobody's Son

You were always cold, Mother
Derides this son, their Telemachus
Who may travel the ancient field of love
Someday in his own halting pauses.

That it is love, not hard breathing and immediate,
Though surely breath is part of the whole
But not resigned either—passionate, middle-aged no doubt

But, yes, passionate, fired not damped by maturity,
Hot in a way that no twenty-year-old
Could understand the source of its steady heat—
If it's bed you want . . .

Almost all of their own age have long given up,
Gone cold before the onset of cold
Who have failed to understand.

Thoughts of old age, even death,
May bank passion in lasting embers,
May even stoke, stroke living warmth from dying flame.

But who has ever thought to define this fervor—
Too late in mortality for Erato to jiggle over it—
Antique, stubbornly monogamous, sturdily dull,

Bound in and to marriage, to the rootbound
Cosmos as well, and utterly free now—
A happier old age for these two old lovers
Whenever the spirit moves.

Demodocus Deposes from a Rocky Hill in Arcadia

But still. The old gods
Were dependable and were even comforting
In their horrifying playfulness
Their glorious lunacy.

An island explodes as we have heard islands have done.
A great ship stands with its stone crew
An obsidian monument to angry water games,
Phaeacia bound by insurmountable cliffs.

We declare the catastrophe an act of the gods
Or one of them
Or the result of a spat between two of them
Or an all-out war amongst them
Or a lunatic act of lordly revenge,

Spite writ cosmic
On some poor lubber after he's been fooled
Into holding his head too high above the sheepfold.

Nobody blamed the gods for any of this, or not much.
The gods did what gods do. Our part wasn't questions.
Our part was to tell the story in a manner
To make grander the Grand,

Make something like wisdom
Out of Athena's night-taloned bitchiness.

Make catastrophe of her diddling Odysseus.
Athens is well endowed with her name and her duplicity,
Her step-child, Plato.

Understand that none of the gods paid attention to subtlety
Or a well turned metaphor, especially
If we were to invent and re-invent as we sang along
And did it fast.

Read Yevtushenko on the subject of *his* gods.
Consider Boswell and Dr. Johnson, David Frost on Nixon
Or university poets angle-writing for grants.
Any press is good, you can hear them struggle to thunder.

So. Thera gets blown to dust, ash,
And flecks of drifting bone,
A drying blood spot here and there.
We don't need to question. The poet invents,
Grabs up his lyre and sings, and sings.

It was never our part
To worry about the state of Theran morality
And worry over what they might have done
That we had better watch ourselves about,

Or share the guilt with fellow sinners,
Or share any guilt, or sin. Our dying was never so petty,
Even the lowly among us, like poets.
Ours was to find a place in the cosmos of stories
To fit it all in, and then some.

It's still the story that counts. Always.
Even for those of us who choose to stay
In the rock-strewn outlands above Tempe
Or Dorset or far Wessex
Munching the simple joys of jujubes and popcorn,
The penny groundlings and our subterranean genius.

We vagabond wag-tongues are the only interlocutors
Between the gods and their human masters.
To remain human without story
Is to resign our shades to politics and hapless faith.

The Wine! . . .

The Ivory Gate

in memory of Louisa and Alfie Waters

Louisa's dead skin is dry, has been for ages now.
Louisa's dead skin mirrors the image of the hand that moves
Not to caress the skin
But almost to shade the skin from its disintegrating
Into discrete mummified cells,
The magic caul her face was swaddled in at birth,
Talisman to entice whatever Odysseus she chose.

Skin, the paper of the old paperback book of modern poems
The poets enticed me to buy when I was a boy.
Skin and paper that
Were I to touch either with a damp finger
Would slough away into the silences that surround them.
Page three hundred and ten, Pound's Seafarer,
Might depart as air
Bequeathed to drift in lacy jags of dust.

Louisa's skin is all of her that remembers now,
Remembers her Odysseus
Gone to sea at fifteen, a long voyage before they met—
Returned as unlettered as he had started out.
Unadventured too, only Alfie Waters.

But not to her!
The skin that touches with lips
The mariner's rope-calloused hands

Heavy with dreary seamanship,
Her pirate prince
Romance of the thousand and second night—
Her Odysseus shipwrecked forever on a Mississippi mud-bar
Selling paper bags from St. Louis to Minneapolis,
Only a river-farer now,
A paying deck-passenger in the day trade
Dares to make money out of new-fangled grocery bags.
Groceries, dry goods, dry soul, Dead Sea
Leached of all but salt.

The oar Tiresias spoke of is only a tool
And his Penelope is his Calypso,
His Circe,
His Scylla,
His wildest disillusionment
Trapped between the storm of her sere disappointment
And the Charybdis of trade—

His own skin nagged
Translucent long before the great age
He could not start to live to.
Translucence is the color of his pain.
Her pain grows on the frail page of my mind
To the many colored splendor of black.

Envoi: Circe Circles

> *a vocational killer*
> *in the machismo of senility*
> Robert Lowell, "Ulysses and Circe"

It's the silk cuts scissors, Cal, in her world, not his,
Not yours, you, alive to any urge but love . . .
To gravity, Nobody awash again in brine and booze,
The drunkard's remorse disguised once more as wisdom,
Volte-face, even in Homer's wood-hulled cosmos.
Would the knowledge have revived you somehow
To know that Homer's man is woman, woman man
For their own good and Homer's, their ship re-keeled,
Fresh sailed, they married not merely "long enough"
But again? Or did you know anyway, and did the knowledge
Overwhelm you, and your woman, your Penelope?
Dolphin drowned in the dust of your dried seabed,
Can you tell siren from siren, your ships burned,
Un-lost friends' weary eyes on your shark's false teeth?

3. Those Who Turned Back from the Mountain

Once I Was a Fist

"How do you know if you're going to die?" . . .
"When you can no longer make a fist."
Naomi Shihab Nye

Once I was a fist,
two of them sparring
indeftly at molecules
in the sheltered sun.

Sometimes when
I look down at my
arthritic old hands
I still hear the tinkle

molecules make when
they twinkle
against the rays
of fading light.

What's left of light
makes what's left
of my warped fist
enough for not dying.

County 40

Two old men in the clinic waiting room
meet once more
maybe one last time for the first time again.

One wears a blue cap with some logo in gold,
the other borne to his plastic chair
by an aluminum walker with tennis ball shoes.

I another old man: a fountain pen.
Blue cap with logo on the chair beside me.
I will not watch, having not been invited,
not been invited either though, not to listen:

Old lady who lived back in there off County 40.
Name was Leona.

Used to be a resort back there. No more.
No more.

We're putting our place up for sale. Moving into town.
Too far from help if you hurt yourself.
Too far if you don't, come to think.

Broke my leg.

The wife broke her wrist.

Yeah well. But if you break your arm you can still walk.
Break your leg you're done.

Now we're all quiet together.

Done.

We're brothers now
maybe thinking about those bones.
Them bones chuckle.
The old health: *them dry bones*, thin dry bones now.
They choose magazines, read at magazines—*Health.*

In honor of our silence,
my age and theirs,
I'm done now too,
with writing not brotherhood.
In brotherhood I rise, *hip bone connected*
to the creak of rejuvenation,

head back up County 40, the winter drive friable
like old drought-soil gone mortally sere—

slick hard treacherous bone-white abyss just under the glare—
back to our family's old house not for sale.

So many things not for sale never seem to be only things.

Emporia Euphoria

In the Sonoran Desert it is nineteen-fifty-five:
nothing but desert dotted with creosote bush,
highway debris and boredom.
I am eleven. Bored.
The flat tan of desert drones by, mile after mile.
The old ones listen to *Monitor* on the car radio.
Then my demure English grandmother:
"Oh! Oh! Look! A *street-walker.*"
The unamused roadrunner fails to get the joke.
My grandmother is embarrassed—
and pleased with the accident of invention
she will tell on herself for decades.

In Kansas, driving toward Emporia:
the sign tells me that I am entering
Flint Hills Country.
I look up from the trance of straight highway
to take in the scenery,
which is pretty much flat, save for the fading sign.
I peel my eyes for hills.
I am no more eager than the comfortable beige landscape
for the climax of gray-flint immensity.
The next sign, a mile and a half behind in a moment,
tells me that I have reached
the summit of Flint Hills Country,
a few feet of elevation above the first sign.
I gasp for what oxygen is left
in the summitized rarification of air.

Down the highway
miles from the sign, from any sign,
my grandmother steps out from behind a creosote bush
back in the Sonoran Desert.
It is nineteen-fifty-five again and still.
She comments on how pretty are the tiny
yellow blossoms. I can
smell in the creosote bush the fragrance of desert rain,
which is always a dry fragrance,
dust subtly perfumed,
and always memory, even minutes after rain stops.
And I smell my grandmother's lavender perfume,
which is really sweet acacia
translated by her memory of some English garden.
I know I am a little delirious now. A little,
with my wealth of sparse scenery.
In the middle of Kansas I slow
to avoid hitting a desert street-walker
in a final moment of this sacred lapse of attention.

Strangers, Maybe

In memory of William Stafford,
whom I have known in words

Allegiances grows softer in my hands,
more comfortable whenever I hold it again.
In between reading old poems again,
in between writing a new poem or two again,
or maybe only a line or only a word, or
something added to the odd collection
of notations I have written in the back of the book,
the old cover, paper over boards, rubbed spine,

recalls the age of old allegiances of my own,
a library smoothing to the touch of re-reading,
but, for just now, only to a handful of books
like this one, and I wonder for a poem's worth,
before I return perhaps to the poem that I have
interrupted writing, or have maybe finished in time
for a thought of those drifting continents
of allegiance, memories reliving wonder—

whether a book that hasn't been written in
is a book, whether a wonder can be
a wonder if it isn't spread out to share.
A poet's love is a book caressed, saved thereby
from the grope of commercial advantage,
read together beyond public distinction—
the true poem, created through time, lived
far beyond the interference of cold redaction.

What you read to the audience that night when
the book was new for the first time, in typescript,
not yet even in print, did not affect me much,
save for a drone of your voice rising obediently
at the end of each small trope. I failed to listen
beyond what seems to me now a quiet discomfort
at performing in the bottled light of remittance.
The crossroad of our attention came later.

We are still strangers, mostly. "The roads go on."
The car you drove, "brown in the snow,"
Carol and I have borrowed all this time and miles
and energy ago "to burrow at the edge, or fall,"
or not fall, and not rise beyond the surface we share
of landscape and road, direction and mis-direction.
We are glad you thought of us. I stir the fire,
but in silence, while we think back of you.

Endlessly Rocking

*For Milo Kline, on his high school graduation tour
Mid-Atlantic, on the way to Africa, 1942*

It wasn't even a storm, just the boat, the *ship*
       rocking. My duffle
             had come unstrapped
       from the bunk and it tried to
roll around
       the deck like a dead
             man (I had not seen a dead man
       yet) or a drunk (I had seen
these, even tried to be
       one that night when even *I*
             had forgotten to write me). It sloshed.
       The boat sloshed. The *ship*!
My mind tried to
       slosh all the way back to the
             sturdy black soil, the green that is
       waveless Iowa. I thought
about the poem in
       the English book, the poem
             before O Captain! My Captain!
       Miss Block had tried to
parse the poet's titles, or
       get us to. Out of the cradle
             endlessly rocking meant rocking
       forever out of the
cradle. Eternally out of
       the cradle. Away from

the cradle. Rocking like
the duffle, helplessly
sloshing. Endlessly
rocking, endlessly,
endlessly. Our fearful
trip . . . the final outing,
the forever of it, before the first fear.

Lost for Good Once More

Thinking of becoming lost,
the small child's feeling
of taloned emptiness in the midst of color,

motherless
like the hermit thrush that has sung
from an invisible jack pine branch.

The thrush will not move from
the same branch while he is singing.
Singing, he is a compass and a joy.

I move from rotting branch to rotting branch
under my feet in a boggy forest
but I will not get lost while the thrush sings.

I will move from black branch to black branch
in the sun-defying forest,
an anthracite sheen of lively decay.

And I cannot become lost, not
into this glow from the lure of darkness visible.
But what if the thrush stops singing?

Answer First, Then Question

1. My Father's Clarinet

He tried to get me to play the clarinet. Not teach—
Not teach. We save our teaching for less worthy
Mortals than sons. Otherwise how could we stand under
The fatal blows, the barrage of our failures.
I learned to play Twinkle, Twinkle, Little . . .

SCREECH!
And the room was attacked by the shrieking pterodactyl,
Greatly taloned leather-winged banshee
That ripped up, devoured the spinal cord
Like vultures at defiant Prometheus' innards.

I have been my petty Prometheus.
Chained wrist and ankle, nailed hand, foot, and ears,
Especially ears, to the cliff wall of the tortured room,
I have refused to account for his graceful gestures
Up and down the black wand of clarinet,

Acknowledge the grace of his notes
As any force greater than magic.
In my father's honor, today I will stuff my raspberry tongue
Back into its wet socket, step away from the wall,
Uncover his ancient Underwood, and tap out

The word, *star,* a signal of the private music he taught me anyway,
To resolve the silent poetry of our difference.
For it is a dishonor, I think now, to believe,
Through the gift of our ordinary failures,
The dark and common creed

That anyone's good skill is only magic or miracle,
Deserving of no more than the puny excuse of awe.
It is a craven way out, not even to emulate, more,
Not to challenge that skill with some resounding force,
At least enough to have offered as his target my gut.

2. Forgiveness

The rhetorical question you ask—unrhetorically—
  "Can forgiving move across generations?"
Well, if some members of the generations are alive,
Maybe—or not, maybe—but why?

Nothing in my poem suggests or hints
Of forgiveness of anyone's father, certainly not mine.
It is possible my father committed
Much that should be forgiven.

But what's the point? He's dead.
And he didn't intend to hurt.
We put the tin of his ashes up there
Behind the window frame,

The "Celestial Seasonings" tin that honors him
With a joke that could have been his.
What we have now is still a relationship.
But the word I used is "resolve,"

And I have much that may be resolved,
But not by him. If I may be blunt,
And for you and your own father I will be,
I hope that my son fails to forgive me

The ills I have committed toward him—
Which I have; I am a father.
I prefer to go to my grave,
Or ashes in my coffee can—

"Chock Full-O-Nuts" would be nice—
Or sifted like flour-dust into the lake,
Having left no issue so awful
As to be forgivable.

But I hope I leave a host of issues
For the next generation to resolve,
Not for forgiveness, maybe not even for peace,
But for all I know of fathers' love.

Moon

The eye of a television
twists toward
a vacant moon
rising into ceiling.

The cat squints toward
rising sunfire
behind its man's
contorted brow.

Together they face
the blank moon
of the empty
living room.

What May Interfere with Sleep

That non-arrangement of pine knots in the beam
I have been looking at from my bed since I was a small child
after my father had forced it up there to support us—
in great inconvenience and trouble and not a little
pain in one shoulder and that bad knee of his—
has always looked to me—

and this is a distraction and an inconvenience to an old man
and lover of peace, or at least decorum—
like a revolver ready to cock, eager to exact such damage
as I shall gladly and finally not miss
in the oblivion that is the absence of the miseries
of the century I was brought to

by birth, rearing, education, and love,
the oblivion that is the absence of
cruelty, war, torture of body, torture of mind,
minds of the imprisoned, the mortally threatened,
the starved for food, for knowledge—brought to
the many moments of the freedom I have squandered.

Oblivion is the absence of consciousness,
the absence of absence, the absence of oblivion.
No distraction
always more and less than whole can be complete.
Distraction can only be *liable* to completion,
never more, never less than grace.

The grace we hunger for in a long life
we find at last may be as painful as faith,
as comforting as doubt.
Still, it is grace, as beautiful as physics,
the distracting tension that keeps us alive:
The shaman's dramatic charm against completion.

I Would Not Care to Die Completed

Last night you were explaining
what you and your busted ankle
require to get you from here to your garden
and the inconvenience this episode has proved to be,
but not the pain.

You added that it was *only* an inconvenience,
not permanent, and that "You learn."
And that's when I thought of something I had written
in the back of some poet's book.
Was it James Wright? Yes—I looked.
"I would not care to die completed," I wrote.

I'd like to see myself lying in my bed
propped up on several down-filled pillows.
My grandmother's—my great grandmother's—
eiderdown comforter is still soft and light.

The air is light, and a glitter of dust motes moves
like a question in the small voice of air, like
angels no bigger than atoms of oxygen.

We share these last hours or moments—
but they, quieter than oxygen released for the occasion
from the head of their infinite kingdom of pin-head

enough voice to breathe soundlessly
that message for stunned Elijah,
for the dying poet too in still small ecstasy
unencumbered by harp or trumpet or even tongue.

The comfortable old doubter is propped on the down pillows,
high enough to remind him not of angelic presences
but of the air that moves them, and moves his breath,
filters his breathing.

There should be flowers, but not inside,
perhaps the usual summer's decorous blue
migration of creeping bellflowers
that work their seasonal way around the house,

not to show themselves off nor to show off the house
but to remind me lying there of their habit
of inhabiting abandoned houses and foundations
and the proper blue gardens of some other century,

gone to seed and mongrel life
that will not stop to be monumental,
never stop nor allow for completion
while I wait for that unnatural punctuation :

out of my control and therefore out of my
range of interests at the ultimate nonce.
I might startle myself away from the communing motes
and the air that lights them and think to myself alone
or maybe ask "What is it?"
and answer or try or pretend.

Yes, pretend—the poet's daily bread—
one breath is never like another.
The task is tasting each
and tasting the silence in the mortal distance between,
and tasting the distance itself.

Her Black Hair

I'm lying on this cold streambank
with my neck arched way back, blank eyesockets
aimed at the midday sun
and I can't hear the water any more
rushing away from this finality of injury.

No, that can't be right
because I am very much alive lying in the midmorning sun
and the wound in my leg really doesn't hurt much.
I caress the bubbling glare of the clear stream
flowing me away from my moment of folly.

So I am lying on my left side then, maybe leaning
on my left elbow so that my pulpy right leg
lies not touching the rough sand.

But that can't be right either because
then I couldn't see her on the edge
of the higher bank that rises in the shade.

So maybe that leg is bleeding away into the creek sand
and downstream
where I need not admit to the sureness of need

because I can see her and she asks
who probably can't see the blood anyway—
is so much of the demand of our manhood always
to conceal the blood?—asks, *Are you all right?*

And I—am I only eighteen here in this story?—
I say *Sure* and I add *Thanks* to her caring face
and I want, oh I want those lips to ask again
and I can tell the real and helpless truth
over and over and maybe forever.

But she leaves my adolescent need forever instead
and forever turns her fine young head of black hair trimmed short
and maybe says OK then and I always hear that
and always she vanishes down stream.
And I will be helped before long, but only up and out.

I only ask her in winter now
and only when the old scars begin to itch or throb,
that old scar on my leg, the scar on the ghost of my heart.

Blue Chords, Blue Clouds

strung out from Moody Blues titles and an homage to Woody

This land is your turnaround backbeat spinning
Cloud of acoustical bass dreaming
Out along the rails the City of New Orleans.
Some wisdom from the ages, some fear. *Some fear!*
Blue loss thrummed out along the rails of wrack-stretched guitar
        string.

Rusted tracks to the other lost chord in search of
Your spectral side of life, your land—
For Proud Mary boiling down the Great River Styx,
Mississippi—holy stream of bent notes cools
Out of flood some fine day, glitters like your blue tomorrows.

Light flies from east to west dawning to dark.
Clouds sail west to east.
Do you ride the light or the clouds?
How is it to ride both at the same time when
We really haven't got time no more, or tempo,

Haven't got time for a past.
Haven't got time for a future passed,
Our blessèd anymores no more.
Fingers and soul tremble through the chords, one of which
May be the lyre note, grace note of salvation. So listen good,

Because this land *is not!* your—
Not our land. This land,
This land *Is*, Boyo, Cowboy, Compañero,
Somewhere here in the poem, the song in blues seven,
Somewhere blue, clear still and always.

The Lady of the Pomegranate

Outside under any shade,
patchwork shadows of mesquite
palo verde or sweet acacia,
deep shade of citrus,
narrow shadows of saquaro and cardón,
arms spread to the seething sky,
spine ceiling of cholla—
the temperature has risen to a hundred and twenty degrees but
inside, the primitive efficiency of swamp cooler
forces the temperature down to seventy-eight
so long as the prosthetic of electricity holds out.

So I will not take my body outside
but to live I will send my arid soul out.
To live, my soul in turn takes me to Earth
past the lizard's crawl-space of cholla
under the healing mystery of creosote bush
and down that narrow hole,
the downward paradise of rattler,
scorpion, tarantula, Teiresias,
down under the sea of baked desert pavement
beneath the concrete of caliche,
down through the magma-cooling unguent of aquifer
until I meet the lady of the pomegranate.

She breaks open the leather of her fruit,
places a single sweet wet bead between my lips,

then another,

then another,

and with each seed I grow that much cooler,

that much warmer.

So cool my lips.

So warm her touch.

Such pure sanity of shelter down,

down,

freed from the restraint of soul

almost ready to return to Earth—

root, branch, thorn, and oh, saguaro's

white blossom, cereus' lure of fecundity,

bats marrying cactus to cactus

in the palpitating heat of the new desert night.

A Gaud for Our Well-Being

My anxiety stares at the dimples
on the skeleton in the doctor's exam room. Dimples.
Really, from the angle I sit, waiting for the skeletal gospel.
Her left arm—
o, yes, these bones compose a she;
look at the demure smile
between her sweet dimples—
hangs naturally, bones of her left palm aligned comfortably
with her leg like you in your warpless health might expect.

But her right arm hangs with the palm hidden backwards,
and I think the fingers are splayed slightly.
Her skull is slanted downward,
her eye sockets aimed toward that right hand,
as though she is admiring the glitter
of a piece of gaudy costume jewelry.
It must be costume, casual on the right hand, don't you think?
Childishly smug,
the smile between the dimples of bone.

It is good to see she has some source of glad gaud left,
standing here futureless,
or hanging assembled, artificially futured,
staring hole-eyed at a bright ring-stone that never was,
who had no more future in the life she bore,
the poverty that made of her a cheap,
subcrafted ivory mobile, hanging here,

than she has in the death she wears about her now,
and her little pride in the big cheap stone. Amethyst?

Perhaps, if I signal her gently,
she will raise her satisfied head,
her smile almost gone into the interruption,
look at me undimpled, serious, human again,
and, after I ask,
gently refuse this dance.
She looks back at the gaudy ring
left her by whom she almost remembers,
and lets me know,

"Better luck next time, sailor. Maybe next time."
And so much future gladdens us both.

If You

If while you are pruning that olive
gently so that what you have in the end
is olive and not much of your ego,
you see a hummingbird nest
so tightly woven of twigs so puny
that only a hummingbird
might find them worth structure
and you see the structure
round and shaped
like a child's best effort at a clay bowl
and only looking, only
touching with your eyes,
you happen to feel the structure,

if indeed you are lucky enough to spot the nest
in the branch you are in a hurry to lop
because it is growing late
in your day's long effort with the tree,
if you see it wedged in the crotch
between two branches so small
that your lopping shears should have missed them
in their sharpened oiled-steel efficiency,
you will stop to admire.

If you happen not to miss seeing
the hummingbird nest, try to
save the whole branch, no matter how big,

how much in the way, how awkward,
but do not forget to come back
to the same olive, even years later.
Surely the nest is gone now
and you can lop the branch so that you
display the olive in your notion of symmetry
then stop once more, hear the same gentle gray hum,
watch for the same gray blur of darting, the same
iridescent throat and notice that
this is the very same hummingbird
although you have not been the same person
for all your careful maturation, your ambitions,
but only if you stop and look for her
so that for the moment of looking you find
that you are nevertheless
and for the spinning wing of the moment
the same steward of the hummingbird's garden,
glad and humble once more
in the promise of that moment and no other.

Miranda's Gift

a cautionary tale for young readers

Miranda gave me the plastic bracelet I am wearing,

Because, she reminds me, some weeks ago
I told the story of an eagle and a tortoise,
Both of which died twenty-four centuries ago, or about.
You know the story. You've been around.
You may have heard it from me, but probably not.

Anyway, it seems that this old Greek playwright—
You remember Aeschylus from high school, right?—
Old Aeschylus, ninety or so years of age,
Was walking in his garden, someone's garden anyway,
Minding his business, maybe working on a play or two,

And, like most of us, not looking up,
Because on the whole we don't look up, do we?
And so, not seeing the eagle that bore the boulder of tortoise
In his talons, where, sky and reptile encumbered,
He had no way to open his lunch—starving amid plenty,

The old poet kept up his old man's ramble,
A stumble or a limp, but so slowly that the eagle missed
The slow show of movement that accompanied
The old poet's bliss, or musings, or agony maybe, or
Maybe savoring what he failed to see was his last promenade.

And the newer old poet who tries to amuse only you,
That old poet, whether he knows it or not,
Will keep company with his precursor, and with Earth and sky
If only to remind him again of all that is in between.
Take this tortoise in both hands, will you? Watch for eagles.

Oh. Did I remember to tell you why? Or what the eagle did next?

Those Who Turned Back from the Mountain

Of course they've failed!
And why not?
The mountain has failed too, is
Failing under the sun

But mostly failing under the rain
That purifies the mountains and the stricken climbers too
In their blessed failures, one day moiled
Into the same good soil as the mountain becomes.

But if they stay
If they make no effort to leave behind
Litchfield, Tempe, Park Rapids, Dorset,
If they miss the mountain entirely

What will they know of gracious failure, of the holy pang of grief
Ah, mostly grief—the grief, partly of course
Of not finishing the hike up
But mostly the grief that makes of the rise, the mountain

Makes of desire, love;
Of breathing, life. Yes
"The fields go on forever, peaceful, beautiful."
But only to the slope of the mountain.

Quotation from "Pastoral," by Louise Glück

Accidence

If Plato is right, are the mists that shine in the blue wind the shadows
Behind the shadows of their shadows, and are they right there
Above the spume of white-capped waves?
The unrhythmic accidence of our insignificant multiple presences:

The Small White, Cabbage White, flutters utterly
Alone out of the blue wind to nibble at the white-capped
Cabbage of waves. The white-capped waves rise to snap
Up the old-bone-white butterfly that flutters out of the blue wind.

This trade is the taste of being
To anything so small, so white, so immense with waves,
So emerged into nameless infinity, and
What is more holy than chastening namelessness?

On the boat's radio we listen to Verdi's Chorus of the Hebrew Slaves,
Free from wordish intrusion smothered in the noise of blue.
Our two-souled ark slues waveward toward the grinding shallows.
We read poetry, fill the ark-void with words.

Memo to the Cabbage White, to the white waves, to the blue wind,
To us reading poetry while our little ark
Chain-dances, soughs with the Hebrew Slaves, echoes in waves
Toward the grinding shadows:

Do not forget what the Franciscan Friar teased, in the blue
Wind of his creative dying,
That "God, after all, is powerless" too,
Not like Plato, blind slave to the boggy hiccups of Reality.

Out of Reality then, the Small White flaps upward
Into the blue wind, flutters into the wind so fast that
She might fly beyond the wind into the mist
That shines through the unshadowed sun.

Our Hands

The exactitude of execution an ancient artist
employs in the details of a bird,
titanium sheen delineated—

and yet we still have trouble depicting hands
(faces too but that is of course)
that are not complicated appendages. So why?

The hand of a young woman over there by the lake
stops painting, brush in midair.
She looks beyond her brush and a wing of fingers.

She seems to look somewhere over the water.
The hand with its brush moves out beyond her attention.
Ah. That's why. The young dancer

knows her moves, watches each part of her body
work in no more than mechanical exactitude. Then her left hand
moves by itself and she follows the grace of it.

Message Returned

to Mary Oliver, whose "work is loving the world"

So is my work loving the world.
For the company of the sunflower,

The clutter of clover that makes my lawn
Unworthy of the word, undeserving of the mower,

And makes beautiful whatever it is instead.

For the company of the hummingbird,
The young crow and the sweetness of his rare, rare silence.

For moss on the shingles, for nameless fungi.
For my blue plums too, the sad, hard, neglected fruit
Next to my father's senile apple tree, fifty years gone.

For the pasture, its gentle abandonment,
Its reforesting maybe only to rude underbrush
Before thistles and fireweed and I leave each other for—

Oh, for blueberries and blueberries,
For weeks bleeding gently among raspberries,

Sweet reddening juice, seeds stuck like
Old Testament signs between my undeserving teeth.

For the phoebe, gray phoebe,
Dull mother of dull fledglings
There on the door sill of the workshop

She and they and I used to share
When we could celebrate each other's residence
By avoiding each other except in her song
My silence.

For all of us who choose to rejoice
In our common, loving disharmonies,
Our awkward share in the love of naked being.

4. Old Poet: New Prologue

Soliloquy by the Candle Light of Day
for Caedmon

I wake up again to clouds—
Clouds, dull linens of clouds
To lines, words of poems
Soft dull linens of words

On the fore and plowing edge of a determined
Raft of dream surging down some sleep-powered wake.
I knew I could wake up—get up
Fumble for one of the pencils on my bedside table

And one of the folded shirt-pocket size
Discarded memories of scarified paper
Write the words or the lines or
Once or twice

Lines of music whose delicacies I cannot notate
Nor ever learned how.
But I knew alerted by the clear spray of ideas now
That I would remember in the morning.

I never did. Did you? Ever?
But one night I dreamt some of those words again
Or lines or prisms of image in the foam of notes.
Then I dreamt that I got up

Got out of bed
Picked up a pencil
Found a folded paper
And then I dreamt that I wrote it all down.

All and beautiful—and all in a murky second gone into the foam.
I've never dreamt such dream again
But some urge behind the surge of dream told me
To write for the fabric of dream, the linen shadows of clouds

Anything at all, anything away from my sullen old silence.
Though it is a grace of old age the dream has been good,
A faith in dreams of embers all these lights ago—the
"Highest candle lights in the dark,"

Which dark
Needs no more than a candle
And less
To read into the wakening heaves of breath a new old life.

www.ingramcontent.com/pod-product-compliance
Lightning Source LLC
LaVergne TN
LVHW091309080426
835510LV00007B/431